How should criminals be sentenced?

OPPOSING VIEWPOINTS PAMPHLETS ®

How Should Criminals Be Sentenced?

This pamphlet is chapter three from *America's Prisons: Opposing Viewpoints*. Other chapters, also available in pamphlet form, are:

What Is the Purpose of Prisons?
How Do Prisons Affect Criminals?
What Are the Alternatives to Prison?

Viewpoints

	Page
Viewpoint One **Selective Imprisonment Should Be Used** *Brian Forst*	92
Viewpoint Two **Selective Imprisonment Should Not Be Used** *Lee S. Pershan*	97
Viewpoint Three **Crime Victims Should Participate in Sentencing** *Louise Gilbert*	103
Viewpoint Four **Crime Victims Should Not Participate in Sentencing** *Wilbert Rideau and Billy Sinclair*	107
A Critical Thinking Skill: Distinguishing Between Fact and Opinion	112
Bibliography	114

The Importance of Examining Opposing Viewpoints

The purpose of this pamphlet, and others in the series, is to confront you with alternative points of view on complex and sensitive issues.

Perhaps the best way to inform yourself is to analyze the positions of those who are regarded as experts and well studied on the issues. It is important to consider every variety of opinion in an attempt to determine the truth. Opinions from the mainstream of society should be examined. Also important are opinions that are considered radical, reactionary, minority or stigmatized by some other uncomplimentary label. An important lesson of history is the fact that many unpopular and even despised opinions eventually gained widespread acceptance. The opinions of Socrates, Jesus and Galileo are good examples of this.

You will approach this pamphlet with opinions of your own on the issues debated within it. To have a good grasp of your own viewpoint you must understand the arguments of those with whom you disagree. It is said that those who do not completely understand their adversary's point of view do not fully understand their own.

A pitfall to avoid in considering alternative points of view is that of regarding your own point of view as being merely common sense and the most rational stance, and the point of view of others as being only opinion and naturally wrong. It may be that the opinion of others is correct and that yours is in error.

Another pitfall to avoid is that of closing your mind to the opinions of those whose views differ from yours. The best way to approach a dialogue is to make your primary purpose that of understanding the mind and arguments of the other person and not that of enlightening him or her with your solutions. One learns more by listening than by speaking.

It is my hope that after reading this pamphlet you will have a deeper understanding of the issues debated and will appreciate the complexity of even seemingly simple issues when good and honest people disagree. This awareness is particularly important in a democratic society such as ours, where people enter into public debate to determine the common good. People with whom you disagree should not be regarded as enemies, but rather as friends who suggest a different path to a common goal.

David L. Bender
Opposing Viewpoints Pamphlets Editor

"Selective incapacitation. . . is in fact a modest proposal for simultaneously confronting the twin demons of high crime rates and large prison populations."

Selective Imprisonment Should Be Used

Brian Forst

Brian Forst is director of research at The Police Foundation, a criminal justice research organization. In the following viewpoint, he supports the criminal sentencing procedure of selective imprisonment, the imprisonment of repeat offenders and dangerous criminals. Selective imprisonment works on the principle that experts can determine which criminals are more likely to commit more crimes and which are not. Those who are more likely to commit crimes are imprisoned for longer periods of time.

As you read, consider the following questions:

1. With selective imprisonment, the author asserts, many who are now in jail would be released. What type of sentencing would they receive?
2. How can selective imprisonment reduce the prison population, according to the author?
3. This type of sentencing is based on predicting future criminal conduct. According to the author, how is future criminal conduct predicted?

The latest prominent principle of sentencing is that of "selective incapacitation." Selective incapacitation, like general incapacitation, involves sentencing with the goal of protecting the community from the crimes that an offender would commit if he were on the street. It differs from general incapacitation in its attempt to replace bluntness with selectivity. Under a strategy of selective incapacitation, probation and short terms of incarceration are given to convicted offenders who are identified as being less likely to commit frequent and serious crimes, and longer terms of incarceration are given to those identified as more crime prone.

Crime Reduction Potential

An attractive aspect of the selective incapacitation concept is its potential for bringing about a reduction in crime without an increase in prison populations. This reduction could be substantial. . . .

The concept of selective incapacitation is controversial, however, for two basic reasons. First, it represents a departure from the more traditional purposes of criminal sanctions—retribution, deterrence, and rehabilitation—purposes that have solid philosophical, if not scientifically validated, foundations. Selective incapacitation is controversial, secondly, because its effectiveness is based largely on the statistical prediction of criminality, and such prediction is an imperfect science. The courts have had great difficulty acknowledging the acceptability of a policy in which its actions are based on imperfect predictions of human behavior, despite the fact that actions of the courts are routinely based on such predictions already in the absence of any such acknowledgment.

Is selective incapacitation truly an effective and appropriate proposal, an "idea whose time has come," or is it another criminal justice fad, or worse—a proposal that carries with it a potential for injustice?. . .

Social Justice and Deterrence

Reserving prison and jail space for the most criminally active offenders may in some instances conflict not only with other norms of legal justice, but with norms of social justice as well. Repeat offenders fall basically into two categories: those who are prone to violence and those who are not. If we reserve the sanction of incarceration only for the dangerous repeat offender, excluding the white collar offender and certain other criminals who pose no serious threat of physical injury to others, we may end up permitting harmful people from the middle class to evade a sanction that less privileged offenders cannot. Some white collar offenders, after all, impose greater costs on society than many dangerous street offenders, and it is clearly unjust to allow the former to pay a smaller price for their crimes than the latter must pay . . . .

For many classes of offenders, a short term of incarceration, indeed, may have a substantially larger crime control impact by way of deterrence than by way of incapacitation. Which offenders? Both empirical evidence and common sense point to the white collar and the property crime offender as the ones who are most deterred by criminal sanctions; the violent offender has been found to be less influenced by the threat of a severe sanction.

Prison for the Dangerous Only

Today's jails are crowded with people who are no threat to anyone—tax cheaters, extortionists, confidence men, stock swindlers, and so forth. They do not belong behind bars. The only reason they are in prison is due to an out-dated and discredited theory that jails "rehabilitate" people.

Nonsense. Let them do their time usefully, outside of jail, nothing cushy but something useful.

This is not a "soft" proposal at all. The dangerous criminals should certainly be shut away. But, today, there often isn't room for the dangerous offender in our overcrowded jails and the dangerous criminal plea-bargains his way back onto the street.

Jeffrey Hart, *The Union Leader*, August 17, 1981.

As long as the offender is a serious, high crime-rate offender, selective incapacitation must obviously be an effective crime control strategy (ignoring crimes against other inmates), regardless of the color of his collar; but it is likely to be a superfluous crime control concept for the offender who is more prone to being individually deterred by a short and usually unpleasant experience in jail or prison. . . .

Effect on Prison Population

What about the prospect of selective incapacitation leading to further prison overcrowding? If, in addition to those who are presently being sent to prison and jail, we were to follow a strategy of incarcerating those with the highest crime-risk profiles, some of whom would not otherwise be incarcerated, then prison and jail populations would indeed be larger than otherwise.

That, however, is not how selective incapacitation works. Under a selective incapacitation strategy, many of those who are currently being incarcerated would receive alternative sanctions—probation with close supervision, the "halfway" house, community service, and so on. Selective incapacitation means reserving prison and jail space for those who are predictably the most criminally active and harmful, subject to maximum and minimum sentence constraints based on offense seriousness. Many who are currently incarcerated would not be under such a strategy. Those who believe strongly in deterrence or just deserts might, indeed, have reason to fear that a strategy of selective incapacitation could cause offenders who they think belong in prison or jail to be released, so that more criminals could go unpunished under that strategy than under other strategies. Thus, larger prison populations might in fact be more closely associated with the deterrence or just deserts strategies than with a selective incapacitation strategy.

It should be obvious that no particular sentencing strategy or mix of strategies is likely to please everyone. Any given prison and jail occupancy level is bound to be too high for some and too low for others. For any given prison population level, however, a selective incapacitation strategy does offer a consistent rationale for attempting to minimize the crime rate.

The Problem of Prediction

One of the most pervasive criticisms of selective incapacitation is that it is based on the statistical prediction of dangerousness; because such predictions are often erroneous, according to this point of view, they should not be used by the court. This criticism is related to both the nature of the errors and to the use of certain information for predicting a defendant's dangerousness.

Let's first consider the nature of errors in prediction. Prediction usually results in some successes and in two kinds of errors: predicting that a phenomenon such as recidivism will occur when in fact it does not ("false positives") and predicting that it will not occur when in fact it does ("false negatives"). The problem of false positives in sentencing is costly primarily to incarcerated defendants who are not really so dangerous, while false negative predictions impose costs primarily on the victims of subsequent crimes committed by released defendants. In predicting whether a defendant will recidivate or "go straight," the problem of false positives is widely regarded as especially serious, for many of the same reasons that it has been regarded in our society as better to release nine offenders than to convict one innocent person. . . .

A tempting alternative is to reject prediction altogether; obviously, if we do not predict, then no errors of prediction are possible. A flaw in this logic is that, whether we like it or not— indeed, even if we tried to forbid it—criminal justice decisions are now, and surely always will be, based on predictions, and imperfect ones, at that. Attempts to discourage prediction in sentencing may in fact produce the worst of both worlds: the deceit of predictive sentencing disguised as something more tasteful, and inferior prediction as well.

If we are to reserve at least some prison and jail space for the most criminally active offenders, then the prediction of criminal activity is an inescapable task. . . .

Selective incapacitation, the latest theory for dealing with crime, is in fact a modest proposal for simultaneously confronting the twin demons of high crime rates and large prison populations. It is less than a universal remedy, first, because our prisons and jails are already populated with many crime prone offenders and, second, because it is not fully consistent with other legitimate reasons to incarcerate some offenders and release others, reasons related primarily to basic principles of justice.

Modest gains, however, are better than none. Continuing frustration with crime on the one hand, and prison and jail overpopulation on the other, suggests a need to exploit modest opportunities whenever they present themselves. Neither the pervasive "career criminal" prosecution programs nor the most touted sentencing guideline systems currently in operation make use of the factors that have been found repeatedly to be associated with repeat criminal behavior. The result is to impose avoidable, and possibly substantial, costs on two groups: offenders who are incarcerated for terms that exceed what can be supported by evidence on how those terms protect the public, and victims of crime committed by released offenders for whom abundant evidence indicates that their release was premature.

Cops and Parole Boards Use It

Some will object to the notion of locking up a 16 year-old rapist or robber for 20 years—until he no longer poses a real threat to the community—by use of a social science derived formula. Yet selective incapacitation has become a working definition for what cops and parole boards are trying to do. In fact, a trickle-down version of the theory—where prosecutors target known career criminals, and judges throw the proverbial book at them—is the best strategy that many communities have devised given scarce resources of cops and prison cells.

Lisa Schiffren, *Policy Review*, Spring 1985.

It is frequently asserted that the public is foolish to insist, simultaneously, on less crime and less taxes for prisons and jails. In fact, less crime may be compatible with less public expenditures on prisons and jails for a variety of reasons. One is the opportunity for prosecutors, judges, and parole boards to make their decisions with a more informed view of the degree of crime risk presented by each defendant.

"Imprisoning an offender because she is dangerous. . . . constitutes an immoral and illegal intrusion upon the individual's freedom."

Selective Imprisonment Should Not Be Used

Lee S. Pershan

Lee S. Pershan is an editor-in-chief of the *New York University Review of Law and Social Change*. In the following viewpoint, Mr. Pershan explains that none of the methods currently used can accurately predict future criminal behavior. People confined under the policy of selective imprisonment may therefore be required to serve unjustly long sentences. Mr. Pershan concludes that it is unlikely that selective imprisonment can provide the benefits that it promises.

As you read, consider the following questions:

1. How does the author prove that predicting criminal behavior is impossible?
2. What does the author mean when he says that selective imprisonment violates the individual's autonomy?
3. How will selective imprisonment affect the crime rate, according to the author?

Lee S. Pershan, "Selective Incapacitation and the Justifications for Imprisonment," *New York University Review of Law & Social Change*, Vol. XII, No. 2, 1983-1984. Reprinted with permission.

Selective incapacitation's opposition to imprisoning the nondangerous offender makes it a seemingly attractive theory. The proponents of selective incapacitation observe that it is unnecessary to imprison the nondangerous, since by definition the nondangerous offender endangers no one. Therefore, penalization should be reserved for those offenders who are likely to commit violent crimes if they are released. Incapacitating the dangerous, it is argued, is the only way to protect the law-abiding public....

Nevertheless, dangerousness is an inappropriate criterion in sentencing proceedings....It is impossible to predict with any accuracy who is likely to prove dangerous. The courts cannot distinguish the dangerous from the nondangerous. In addition, because the definition of violent crime will undoubtedly exclude most dangerous corporate crime, many dangerous offenders will remain free....Even if it were possible to identify the dangerous offender, it would be impermissible to incarcerate her on the grounds that she was dangerous. Imprisoning an offender because she is dangerous is punishment based on status and future behavior. It constitutes an immoral and illegal intrusion upon the individual's freedom....

Attempts to Identify the Dangerous

The most fundamental practical problem with selective incapacitation is the inability of the courts to determine which offenders are dangerous. Although different approaches...have been used, no one has been able to identify the dangerous offender. It is essential to note that the issue here is the prediction of *future* dangerousness, not the assessment of *past* acts. Therefore, even if the sentencing judge knows that the offender was dangerous when she committed the crime for which she is being sentenced, that judge cannot know whether or not the offender remains dangerous and will commit a crime if she is released.

The difficulty in predicting future dangerousness is evident from follow-up studies of offenders who have been diagnosed as dangerous by courts, parole boards, psychiatrists and social workers. In every study, the majority of these supposedly dangerous offenders has failed to act true to form; only a small minority has committed more offenses. Those incorrectly diagnosed (i.e. those who did not, contrary to predictions, commit any more crimes) have invariably outnumbered those correctly diagnosed (i.e. those who upon release did commit more crimes), sometimes by as much as eight to one. Thus, when an offender is incapacitated for being dangerous, most of the time incapacitation is unnecessary—the offender is no longer dangerous. In an extreme case, only 5.2% of a group of supposedly dangerous juvenile offenders offended anew. This is more aptly called "unselective incapacitation." If incarceration is appropriate only for the dangerous, then most imprisoned offenders have been unjustly incarcerated. . . .

If incarceration is to be based on the courts' current ability to predict dangerousness, almost as many dangerous offenders will be released as imprisoned. If the goal of selective incapacitation is to protect the public from the dangerous offender, it is necessary to make more accurate predictions. . . .

Past Actions May Not Be Relevant

Determining that the offender has proven dangerous in the past does not tell the court whether or not the offender currently presents a high risk to the public. There is no logical reason to assume that since the offender has committed a violent crime in the past, she will commit more violent crimes in the future. Such definitions based on past behavior are both too broad—since offenders who are unlikely to offend again are incarcerated along with those who are likely to re-offend—and too narrow, since those offenders who have so far only been convicted of nonviolent crimes will be labelled non-dangerous even if they are highly likely to commit violent crimes in the future. . . .

Selective Imprisonment and the Courts

If psychiatrists and psychologists are ready to concede that they cannot predict which offenders will prove dangerous and which will not, judges who have not had training in prognosticating the future behavior of offenders should not use dangerousness as a factor in sentencing proceedings. . . .

Prediction Is Unpredictable

Predictably, the idea of selective incapacitation is attractive to many politicians and law enforcement people. . . .

But the problems are many and have not begun to be adequately addressed. The theory poses a serious threat to one of the basic precepts of criminal law: innocent until proven guilty. Selective incapacitation metes out punishment for predicted future crimes. And the study of predicted behavior, whether it be violent and dangerous, or merely recidivist, is an inexact science at best.

Jericho, Winter 1982/83.

It is not surprising that courts have had difficulty predicting dangerousness. It is probably impossible to provide a definition of dangerousness that will separate the nondangerous from the dangerous so that a court can determine whether the offender needs to be incapacitated. Classifications must assume that people will invariably act in character, but chance and circumstance lead people to behave out of character. No prediction is perfect. Consequently, attempts to punish on the basis of dangerousness must founder because the court is forced to guess whether or not the offender is dangerous. . . .

No Accurate Predictions

In conclusion, the studies indicate that at present it is impossible to make accurate predictions of dangerousness. For every offender correctly labelled dangerous, at least one offender will be erroneously labelled dangerous. If the number of mistaken predictions of dangerousness is significantly reduced so that the predictions of dangerousness are correct even fifty percent of the time, there will still be several mistaken predictions of nondangerousness for every correct prediction of dangerousness. Nor do the studies offer much hope for improvement. Many conclude that it will never be possible to identify the dangerous. Therefore, since half the dangerous offenders will slip by—they will not be incarcerated—and many nondangerous offenders will be imprisoned mistakenly, bifurcating punishment according to an assessment of dangerousness is unjust. . . .

Selective Incapacitation and the Crime Rate

Although sentencing policies generally are not expected to have any effect on crime rates, proponents of selective incapacitation argue that it should be adopted precisely because it will reduce the crime rate without increasing the prison population. By selectively imprisoning dangerous offenders, the streets will supposedly be made much safer for law-abiding citizens. However, selective incapacitation's effect will not be nearly as great as its proponents suggest. . . .

Incapacitating an individual prevents that person from committing a crime so long as she is imprisoned. However, if the offender is not permanently incarcerated, she is not permanently incapacitated. Most offenders will eventually be released even if they remain dangerous, as the proportionality requirement will usually preclude permanent incapacitation.

Selective incapacitation, therefore, is a practical method of crime prevention only if prisons rehabilitate. Unfortunately, prisons do not (and perhaps cannot) rehabilitate. Rehabilitation is especially unlikely to work in the currently overcrowded and lawless prisons. When the inmate leaves prison, most likely she has not been reformed.

In fact, in many cases prisons make prisoners more dangerous. . . .

If the ordinary (i.e., nondangerous) offender is prepared (or forced by circumstances) to resume a criminal career, it is especially likely that the dangerous offender—who was incarcerated precisely because it was certain that she would commit a violent crime if she was not imprisoned and who was not paroled because she remained dangerous—will soon offend again. In fact, if she did not, the assessment of dangerousness would have been wrong, and the premise upon which incapacitation was justified would be invalid. . . .

Violent Crime Will Not Cease

With selective incapacitation violent crime will not cease. Many violent crimes are committed by people with no record of violence. Under a selective incapacitation scheme at the time of this violent offense they would not have been incapacitated since, if they had previously committed any crimes, those crimes would be minor ones. Nor, if they are unlikely to commit more violent crimes in the future, will they be incarcerated for this crime. . . .

Selective incapacitation may actually lead to an increase in crime. If one believes that offenders are deterred by the certainty of punishment, especially the certainty of imprisonment, selective incapacitation is counterproductive since the likelihood of imprisonment decreases. The offender, who currently does not know if she will be caught, or prosecuted, or convicted, will face one more uncertainty: she will not know whether she will be labelled dangerous or nondangerous. Because fewer offenders will be imprisoned, offenders may be readier to commit crimes. . . .

The Selective Imprisonment Myth

We do not know whether keeping certain convicted robbers and burglars locked up will have any impact on the rates of robbery and burglary. Nonetheless, the return of [this] old myth is getting a lot of attention. It always does, because it is such a convenient answer to the crime problem. It focuses on some of the least powerful persons in the society and makes no demands of the status quo.

John K. Irwin, *The California Prisoner*, May 1983.

Selective incapacitation's rhetoric is direct: rehabilitation did not work, deterrence did not work, retribution is not working. Therefore, only selective incapacitation is left; let's try it. . . . Selective incapacitation is founded upon despair; it is the proposal of a bankrupt. The proponents have retreated to the position that even though the threat of imprisonment will not deter people outside prison, not even those who have just been released, and even though incarceration does not reform criminals, imprisonment is beneficial. It is beneficial not because of any satisfaction that law-abiding citizens may obtain when they hear the news that an offender is to be deprived of her liberty and locked in a cell with other equally vile offenders, but merely because while the offender is locked behind bars, she cannot commit any more crimes.

Incapacitating offenders, however, must also be rejected as a justification for incarceration. Because the dangerous offender cannot be identified, incapacitation will prove unselective. There will be either arbitrary incapacitation or general (i.e., total) incapacitation. The implementation of selective incapacitation is unlikely to reduce prison overcrowding or reduce the cost of running prisons. Because selective incapacitation punishes for future acts, implementation of this theory may be unconstitutional and it clearly is incompatible with the right of autonomy. Nor is it evident that it will reduce street crime. . . .

A careful analysis suggests that selective incapacitation should be rejected. First, it is impossible to identify the dangerous offender. As a result, either the vast majority of offenders are imprisoned to insure that all dangerous offenders are incarcerated or a small number of offenders is imprisoned so that most of the non-dangerous offenders will not be imprisoned mistakenly. If the former policy is followed, the prison population will rise and over-crowding will increase. If the latter policy is followed, many dangerous offenders will not be imprisoned and, if the proponents of selective incapacitation are correct, the crime rate should rise.

Moreover, any attempt to make imprisonment turn on a finding of dangerousness involves ethical and constitutional difficulties. The dangerous offender is imprisoned not for her past acts, but for her predicted future acts and for being "dangerous." Since one cannot be punished for one's status or for still-unattempted acts, selective incapacitation rests on constitutionally infirm ground. Moreover, the offender's autonomy is denied when she is told that she will commit a crime, despite all her protests to the contrary.

Finally, it seems unlikely that selective incapacitation can provide the benefits that it promises. The crime rate is unlikely to go down. The prison population will remain at least as large as it is today.

3

"Victims . . . should be consulted about charges, plea bargains and tactics."

Crime Victims Should Participate in Sentencing

Louise Gilbert

A relatively recent development in criminal sentencing is the participation of crime victims in all aspects of the sentencing process: bail, original court sentence, and future parole and probational hearings. In the following viewpoint, Louise Gilbert gives a powerful first-hand account of the brutal murders of her son and daughter-in-law and her own abortive attempt to be involved in the legal proceedings against the killer. In doing so, she makes a strong case for allowing crime victims' testimony.

As you read, consider the following questions:

1. Do you feel that Ms. Gilbert was treated justly by the criminal justice system? Why or why not?
2. Why does Ms. Gilbert believe that she should have been allowed to participate in the sentencing of her son's murderer?

The scene is a tree-lined main street in a small Southern town. It is deceptively quiet. My family and I are the only strangers. We are victims. I am a victim of the violent murder of my son and daughter-in-law.

Andy and Pamela moved from suburban Philadelphia south, from manicured lawns to an 80-acre farm with a log house in need of restoration. They had seen those peaceful hills on their honeymoon only one year earlier and decided it was the perfect place to raise children and build their lives. Their dreams ended on June 24, 1981. Pam was beaten, raped and shot, wrapped in a blanket and buried in the cistern behind their house. That night Andy was shot in the back of the head. The man who would subsequently be charged with their murders was an acquaintance of theirs.

The first trial was scheduled for October and postponed, rescheduled for December. I had to go. It was my responsibility to represent Andy and Pam. I would be evidence of their having been alive and loved. The trial was postponed again at the request of the defense. It became apparent we, as parents, had no legal identity.

Decomposing Bodies

Finally in February we sat, with my eldest son, in a small courtroom. I met the prosecutor and moments later came face to face with the man charged with killing my children. During the trial, I learned the full meaning of horror as their last hours were never again left to my imagination. Pam's fractured head and almost nude body were described in detail as well as the size of the maggots and flies that covered her. I bolted the courtroom when the pathologist began to describe my son's bloated body.

The courtroom was a battlefield, combat played out between lawyers and judge with a calm defendant dressed in his best. In life Andy and Pam were young and hopeful, in love with life and each other. Their home was an investment in the future, left half completed. To the defense it was a rough cabin in the woods, a dark question asked over and over: "Why were they there?"

Pam's blood was found in the back of the accused's car. His body, head and pubic hair were found on the blanket in which she was wrapped. After being identified near the scene of the crime the day they were killed, he gave out this story: he and Pam were having an affair. Who could dispute this? Not Pam. More than 90 pieces of evidence were introduced by the prosecution. The defense attacked the method of investigation. Out for three days, the jury reported a deadlock; courtroom gossip had it at 11-1 for conviction. A new trial date was set for August 1982.

Planning for the second trial became our obsession. This time we hired an attorney to represent us. She wanted transcripts. We spent a small fortune to transcribe 1,600 pages of testimony. Meanwhile, the prosecutor lost his bid for re-election and the trial was postponed. We paid for our attorney to go south to discuss the case.

Reprinted by permission. Tribune Media Services Inc.

With the same evidence and witnesses, the case was presented differently. I thought it was a good prosecution and a good jury. But then, after two days of deliberations, an emotional jury returned to the courtroom. It was hopelessly deadlocked. One old man said he had not heard all the evidence: he had a "hearing problem," something he did not mention before the alternates were discharged. Some jurors sobbed: the newspaper reported that even the judge choked back tears. A mistrial was declared and a new trial date was set.

We are financially secure but not wealthy. Preparations to attend these trials were made at great inconvenience and expense. We were at the mercy of schedules made, broken and remade. I was depressed, anxious and in therapy.

Finally, more than two years after the murders, the third trial began in the same courtroom, in the same small, rural community that had been subjected to rumors about my children. By law, a change of venue is left to the discretion of the defense.

Andy and Pam were lost to us, and their character and dignity were lost in the courtroom. Because of the system, the prosecutor was never allowed to be an advocate for them and the defense attorney's attacks were never answered. The trial was over in five days. This time the jury was out and back in what seemed like an hour. Their verdict: not guilty.

Justice System Failed

The case is still open, but it is over for us. The structure of our family was blown apart. Piece by piece we are trying to put ourselves together. I belong to Parents of Murdered Children. Our stories are different but the agony is the same. One pattern is repeated again and again: for us the criminal-justice system has failed to work.

The parents, spouse and children of a murder victim are victims too, and their willingness to become involved should be shored up with legislation and changes in court practice. Victims should have a say in choice of venue and whether hearing dates are continued. Victims should be given free copies of court transcripts. They should be consulted about charges, plea bargains and tactics. They should be informed of the progress of the case. If all else fails, they should be provided with a legal advocate who is permitted to defend the character and the integrity of the dead.

My rights as a parent were no less important than the defendant's. I was victimized by the murder of my children. Then the system victimized me again.

"In some instances crime victims—and the organized groups supporting their cause—have resorted to tactics designed to control and intimidate the justice system."

Crime Victims Should Not Participate in Sentencing

Wilbert Rideau and Billy Sinclair

The Angolite is one of the best inmate prison publications in the nation. It is published by the inmates of the Louisiana State Penitentiary in Angola, Louisiana, and is edited by lifers Billy Sinclair and William Rideau. In the following viewpoint, the editors of *The Angolite* believe that crime victims' participation in criminal sentencing borders on the vengeful. Rather than seek justice, crime victims merely try to sway judges and juries toward longer sentences.

As you read, consider the following questions:

1. Why do the authors believe that crime victims do not act responsibly?
2. What are the authors trying to prove when they cite the case of Tony Cimo?
3. What danger do crime victims groups pose, according to the authors?

Too often in the past victims of crime have been neglected and even abused by the workings of the criminal justice system. However, in recent years crime victims, as well as their families and supporters, have been more assertive of their interests, carving out a legitimate role in the justice system. But in some instances crime victims—and the organized groups supporting their cause—have resorted to tactics designed to control and intimidate the justice system rather than make it function properly and equitably.

In Detroit Judge Charles Kaufman presided over the trial of two men, Ronald Ebens and his stepson Michael Nitz, who were charged in connection with the beating death of Vincent Chin. Chin was beaten to death with a baseball bat outside a suburban Detroit tavern where he had been celebrating his coming marriage. Ebens and Nitz, both of whom are blue collar workers with no prior criminal history, entered into a plea bargain and pled no contest to a charge of manslaughter. They were fined $3,780 each and placed on three years probation.

Refusing to Buckle

There was an immediate outrage by Chin's family who felt the sentence was too lenient. A group called American Citizens for Justice, a group composed mainly of Asian-Americans, organized a protest rally against Kaufman, demanding that he change the sentence and jail Ebens and Nitz. Despite the protests and criticisms, Kaufman refused to buckle under the demands, saying in a written opinion: "While sympathizing with the family and community of the victim, it is the obligation of the court to decide the matters in accordance with the mandate of law."

But in Denver Judge Alvin Lichtenstein couldn't handle the pressure of protest. He had sentenced Clarence Burns to serve two years in a work-release program for the shooting death of his wife, Patti. In sentencing Burns, Lichtenstein stipulated that he could continue working at his $850-a-month job and would serve his sentence at nights and on weekends in jail so that he could support his teenage son. The sentence stirred such a storm of protest that even Gov. Richard Lamm injected himself in the storm of controversy by calling the sentence "an outrage" and his wife added that the sentence meant women in Colorado are nothing more than property.

What particularly incensed some of the protesters, especially the women's groups, was Lichtenstein's unfortunate remark that Mrs. Burns helped "provoke" her own death by pretending her marriage was stable. As the noise of the crowd pounded in his ears, Lichtenstein changed the sentence to four years in prison, saying that he had been misled by lawyers. Even the stiffer sentence was criticized by the women's groups, prosecutors and defense attorneys.

Lichtenstein justified his change of mind by saying that he learned that Mrs. Burns had left her son nearly $100,000 in assets.

That "eliminates the very foundation on which the (original) sentence was imposed," Lichtenstein told Burns. "Neither the prosecution nor your lawyers informed me before I imposed sentence that this large sum of money was available to your son for his immediate support and for his college education. Quite frankly, I believe the court was misled."

Caving into Pressure

David Wyman, Burns' public defender, objected to the sentence, saying that Lichtenstein caved in to "continuing pressure from the media and the public."

Victims Trespass on Criminal Rights

Victims' rights do not have to trespass on the civil liberties of us all. Without absolving the individual perpetrator from his/her actions, society must also be held accountable for the environment in which such crimes are committed. Alternatives to incarceration can emphasize the rights of the victim alongside the responsibility of the offender. But the community must be willing to create and implement such alternatives.

Efforts aimed at making the defendant suffer to the same extent as did the victim is not justice. It is the voice of angry and scared people who do not feel that they have been heard. Furthermore, it is only too easy for the Right to capitalize on the emotions generated by the movement for victims' rights.

Jericho, Spring 1983.

A group in Houston called CRIME (Crime Reduction Involvement Means Education) tried to intimidate Judge Woody Densen. Supporters of the group placed at least 100 calls to the court saying that they wanted 18-year-old Tyrone Carmouche, a convicted burlgar, to be given a stiff sentence. Defense counsel Howard Stripling moved for a mistrial, arguing that his constitutional rights had been violated by CRIME's efforts to influence the judge's sentence. Following a hearing on the motion, Densen ordered a new trial and removed himself from the case, saying that he could no longer be fair and impartial in the case. "This group adversely affects the criminal justice system," Densen said from the bench. He called upon the press, defense lawyers and prosecutors to look into the methods employed by that group, charging that the group seems to target certain judges and conducts itself like a political organization. . . .

Public distrust of the criminal justice system, especially the role of the courts, has spawned law-and-order and court monitoring groups throughout the country. Judges, lawyers, and even some prosecutors are growing uneasy with the pressure tactics being utilized by these groups to impose their concepts of justice on the system. Despite warnings by lawyers and judges that it could clog the courts and perhaps be eventually declared unconstitutional, voters in California last year approved by 56 percent to 44 percent a referendum popularly known ''as the crime victim's bill of rights.'' California is also the state that produced MADD—Mothers Against Drunken Drivers—which now has 153 chapters with 75,000 members across the country. At a recent meeting of 20 Municipal Court Judges in San Francisco it was disclosed that the San Mateo chapter of MADD was monitoring their courtrooms. . . .

It is not so much that judges, lawyers and prosecutors are intimidated by the presence of the groups in the courtrooms, but that they feel the groups should conduct themselves responsibly. Some members of these groups do not know how to criticize responsibly; they wish to set themselves up as divine arbitrators of right and wrong and forcefully impose their views, often articulated with reckless abandon, upon the justice system. They enter the courtroom with presupposed notions as to the guilt of the accused—and once guilt is established through a formal verdict, they expect a harsh and quite often maximum sentence without the benefit of the sentencing information a judge has. . . .

Out for Revenge

A basic problem with the organized monitoring groups is that they fashion their concepts of justice in their living room meetings; concepts which are not thought out or well-reasoned. These groups are primarily angry and dissatisfied with the justice system, but rather than seek changes of the system through the elective and legislative process, they seek to change the system through pressure and intimidation.

Of course, an underlying danger in these groups is that their actions will spark a Tony Cimo—a man who waited four years for the State of South Carolina to execute the killer of his parents before he took the law into his own hands. The justice system moved too slowly for Cimo's concept of justice—he wanted immediate revenge, and when he didn't get it, he hired convicted mass murderer, Donald ''Pee Wee'' Gaskins, to place a booby-trapped intercom in the death cell of Rudolph Tyner, the killer of Cimo's parents. Tyner was killed when Gaskins detonated the intercom. ''It had to be done,'' the 36-year-old Cimo said. ''It's something that should have been done.''

At his sentencing Assistant Solicitor Richard Harpootlian said: ''Tony Cimo is a tragic figure. He's even more tragic now.'' Judge James Morris, before passing sentence, said, ''People cannot take the law into their own hands.''

That fact did not disturb a lot of law-abiding citizens who hailed Cimo as a folk hero. ''We've had a bunch of phone calls from all over," Cimo said. "Everyone has been sympathetic...well-wishers. They all feel the same way I do...."

Stirring Up Anger and Frustration

And therein lies the basic danger of monitoring groups—they stir frustration and resentment against the justice system which can prompt the irresponsible individual to take the law into his own hands. America has a lynch-law history; it's an evil that lurks in its soul and Cimo is an expression of the evil, something Wolfe called a "naked worship of brute force." The Cimos want to impose their own concepts of justice with brute force; theirs are the disguised voices of barbarians. They want to dismantle the orderly process of justice; they want to respond to murder with murder. More than a tragic figure, Cimo is a dangerous symbol—he is a murderer as much as Rudolph Tyner was a murderer and ten million well-wishing calls will not erase that fact—it simply bespeaks the dangerous and disturbing trend which is now attacking the very fabric of our justice system.

Distinguishing Between Fact and Opinion

This activity is designed to help develop the basic reading and thinking skill of distinguishing between fact and opinion. Consider the following statement as an example. "Overcrowding is a serious problem in many of America's prisons." This statement is a fact with which few women, men, or government officials would disagree. But consider a statement which attributes prison overcrowding to poverty. "The increase in poverty has driven more people into criminal activity—leading to an increase in prison overcrowding." Such a statement is clearly an expressed opinion. A poor person who has robbed a grocery store to feed his family may agree with this statement, but another equally poor person holding a full-time job may resent the assumption that the poor turn to crime.

When investigating controversial issues it is important that one be able to distinguish between statements of fact and statements of opinion.

The following statements are taken from the viewpoints in this chapter. Consider each statement carefully. *Mark O for any statement you feel is an opinion or interpretation of facts. Mark F for any statement you believe is a fact.*

If you are doing this activity as a member of a class or group, compare your answers with those of other class or group members. Be able to defend your answers. You may discover that others will come to different conclusions than you. Listening to the reasons others present for their answers may give you valuable insights in distinguishing between fact and opinion.

If you are reading this book alone, ask others if they agree with your answers. You too will find this interaction very valuable.

$$O = opinion$$
$$F = fact$$

1. Prison sentences are for punishment.
2. Selectively imprisoning criminals can reduce crime.
3. A small percentage of criminals commit a large percentage of crime.
4. Selective incapacitation means reserving prison and jail space for those who are the most criminally active and harmful.
5. It is impossible to predict which criminals will commit more crimes.
6. Criminal sentencing, as it is practiced now, involves a lot of guesswork.
7. It is impossible to have less crime and fewer prisons.
8. Imprisoning dangerous offenders because they are dangerous is immoral and illegal.
9. Incapacitating criminals, or making sure they won't commit more crimes by locking them up, should not be a purpose of prison.
10. Privately-operated prisons can save money.
11. Restitution is an alternative to prison.
12. There are about two dozen privately-operated prisons in the US.
13. Criminals should suffer as much as their victims.
14. Crime victims may feel vengeful toward the criminals who victimized them.
15. Society must punish murderers.
16. Crime victims can stir frustration and resentment against the justice system.
17. Corporal punishment is used in many third world countries.
18. Electric shock is a more humane punishment than prison.
19. Laboratory research on rats has shown that electric shock is an effective punishment.
20. Chronic pain is not as effective as acute pain.
21. The military needs men, and society needs new solutions to prison overcrowding.
22. Military conscription can aid criminals' reintegration into society.
23. Restitution has been employed throughout history.
24. Restitution is less restrictive than imprisonment.

Bibliography

The following list of books, periodicals, and pamphlets deals with the subject matter of this chapter.

Jan M. Chaiken and Marcia R. Chaiken	*Varieties of Criminal Behavior*, Santa Monica, CA: The Rand Corporation, 1982.
Congressional Digest	"Federal Criminal Sentencing Policy," June/July 1984.
Francis J. Flaherty	"Crime and Punishment," *The Progressive*, September 1984.
Peter W. Greenwood	*Selective Incapacitation*, Santa Monica, CA: The Rand Corporation, August 1982.
Kenneth Guentert	"Stop Punishing Criminals," *U.S. Catholic*, June 1983.
Robert Hanley	"Listening to the Woes of the Victimized," *The New York Times*, October 23, 1984.
Philip W. Harris	"Sentencing Alternatives: Development, Implementation, Issues and Evaluation," *Judicature*, December/January 1985.
Arthur Johnson	"A Barometer of Violence," *Macleans*, March 5, 1984.
Gaylen Moore	"The Beast in the Jungle," *Psychology Today*, November 1983.
Newsweek	"Giving Victims a Say in Court," March 14, 1983.
	"Sentence by Public Opinion," March 5, 1984.
Prison Fellowship	"Liberty to the Captives," *The Other Side*, December 1981.
Science News	"Predicting Dangerousness: Future Imperfect," June 9, 1984.
Society	"Setting Prison Terms," July/August 1984.
Jackson Toby	"A Higher Price for Lesser Crimes," *The Los Angeles Times*, February 24, 1984.
U.S. News & World Report	"When Convicted Killers Walk Free," January 16, 1984.
	"Crime Victims Ask for Their Day in Court," February 7, 1983.

This pamphlet is a chapter taken from a book in the OPPOSING VIEWPOINTS SERIES. It is only one of many available titles. The pamphlets help readers become more intelligent and discriminating consumers of information in our media-centered culture. The pamphlets use magazines, journals, books, and newspapers, as well as statements and position papers from a wide range of individuals and organizations. The discussion activities are designed to help develop basic reading and thinking skills.

Those
who do not know
their opponent's arguments
do not completely understand
their own.

Greenhaven Press

P.O. Box 289009
San Diego, CA 92128-9009